T.M.S.
2-10
Foll
12.86
LB

D0987234

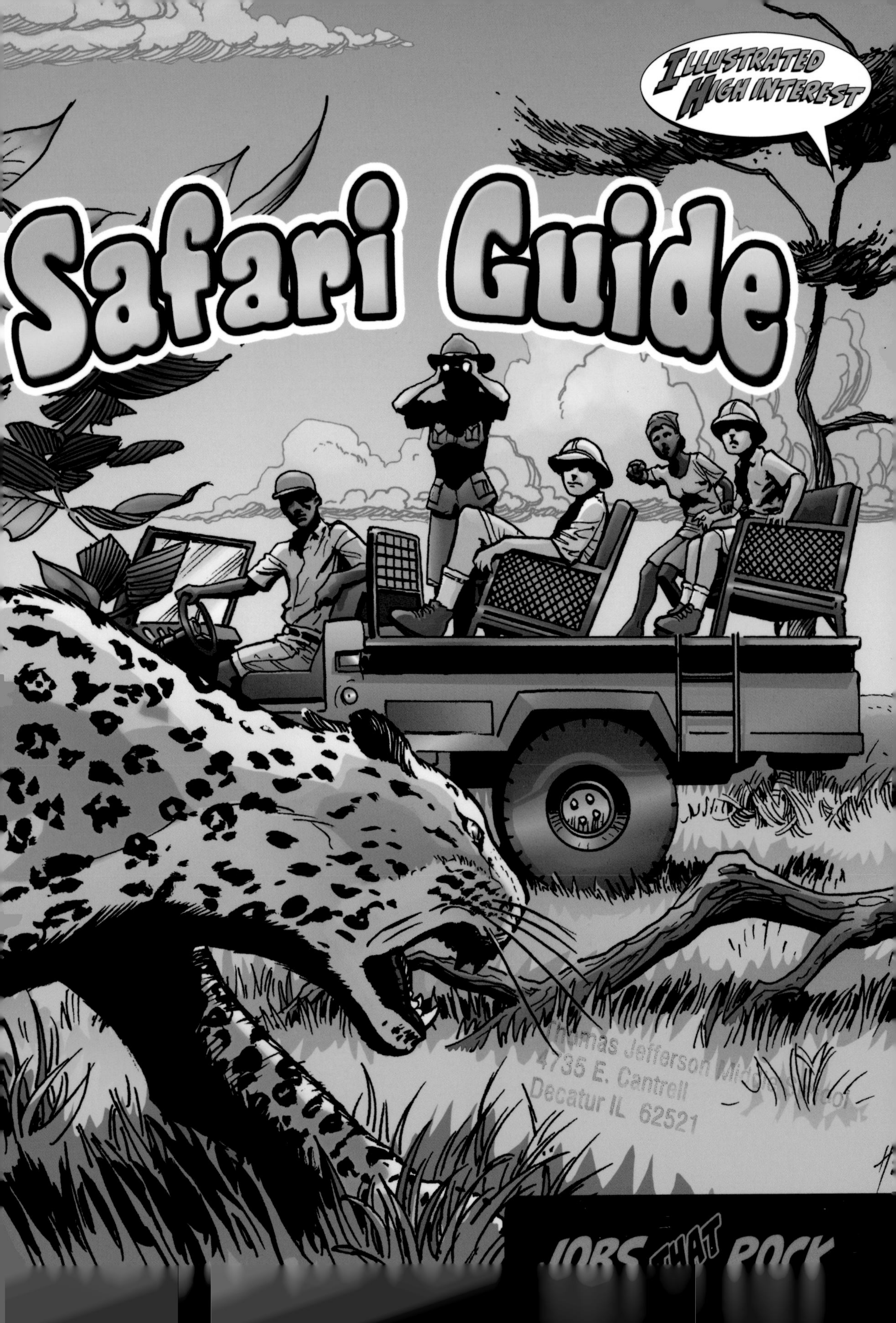
Illustrated High Interest
Safari Guide
Jobs That Rock

Safari Guide

By Tim Clifford
Illustrated By Ken Hooper
Colored By Lance Borde

ROURKE PUBLISHING

Vero Beach, Florida 32964

www.rourkepublishing.com

Edited by Katherine M. Thal
Illustrated by Ken Hooper
Colored by Lance Borde
Art Direction and Page Layout by Renee Brady

Photo Credits: WltR, minny © pg. 1, 4, 5, 26-32; Berrit_de_Vries, rhardholt, Benjiecce, Jimclark1947, cworthy © pg. 26; GJohnsonz, Andrejsegorous © pg. 28

Library of Congress Cataloging-in-Publication Data

Clifford, Tim, 1959-
 Safari guide / Tim Clifford.
     p. cm. -- (Jobs that rock graphic illustrated)
  Includes bibliographical references and index.
  ISBN 978-1-60694-372-4 (Hardcover) (alk. paper)
  ISBN 978-1-60694-555-1 (Softcover)
  1. Wildlife watching--Africa--Comic books, strips, etc. 2. Wildlife watching--Africa--Juvenile literature. 3. Safaris--Africa--Comic books, strips, etc. 4. Safaris--Africa--Juvenile literature. 5. Safari guides--Africa--Comic books, strips, etc. 6. Safari guides--Africa--Juvenile literature. I. Title.
  QL336.C55 2010
  591.96--dc22
                                        2009020482

Printed in the USA
CG/CG

3 7549 00014 4405

ROURKE PUBLISHING

www.rourkepublishing.com - rourke@rourkepublishing.com
Post Office Box 643328 Vero Beach, Florida 32964

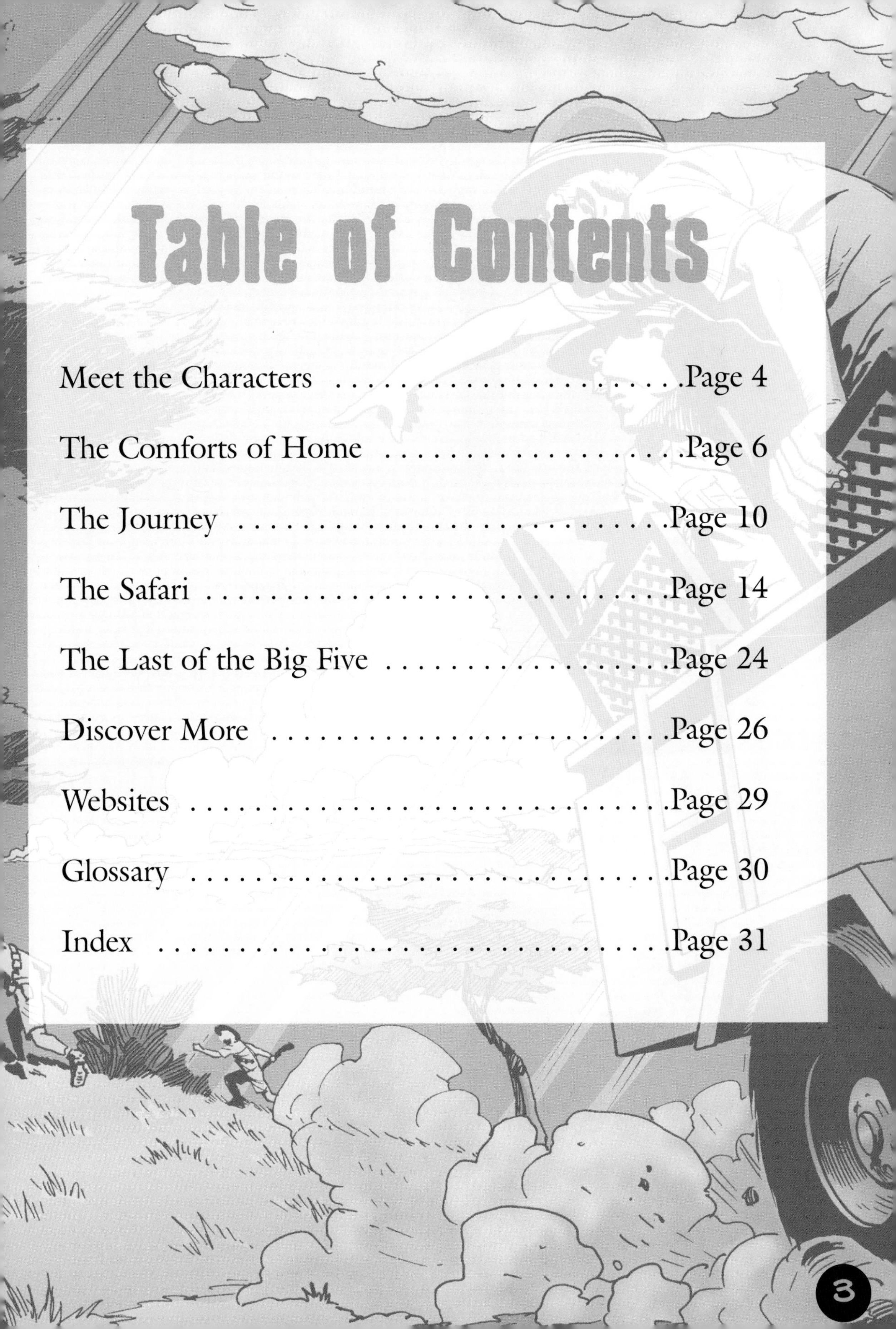

Table of Contents

Imamu

Imamu is a Kenyan Safari Guide.

Zuri

Zuri is Imamu's 12-year-old daughter.

Mr. Williams

Mr. Williams is Parker's father.

Mrs. Williams

Mrs. Williams is
Parker's mother.

Parker

Parker is Mr. and Mrs.
Williams 12-year-old son.

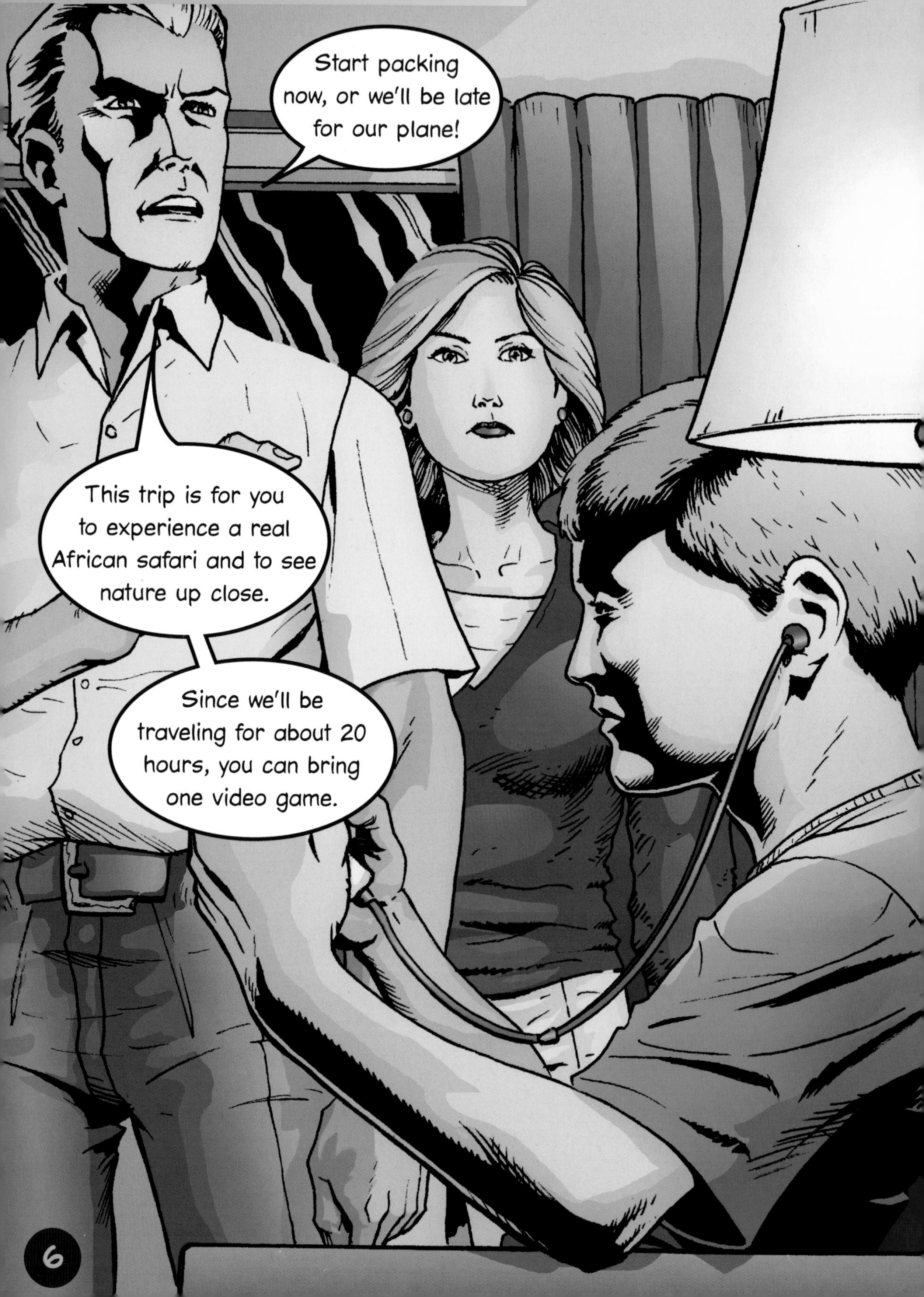
Start packing now, or we'll be late for our plane!
This trip is for you to experience a real African safari and to see nature up close.
Since we'll be traveling for about 20 hours, you can bring one video game.

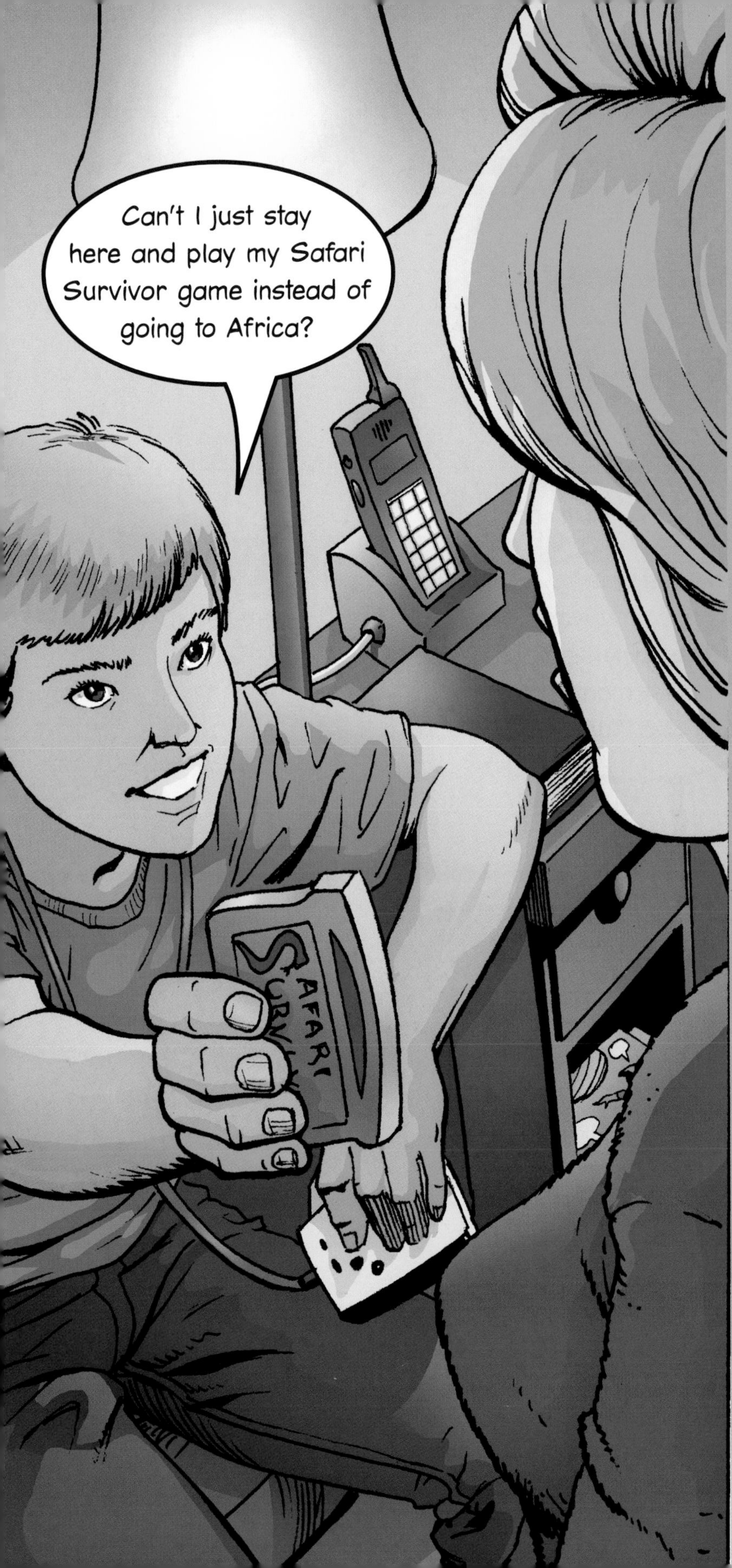
Can't I just stay here and play my Safari Survivor game instead of going to Africa?
SAFARI SURVI

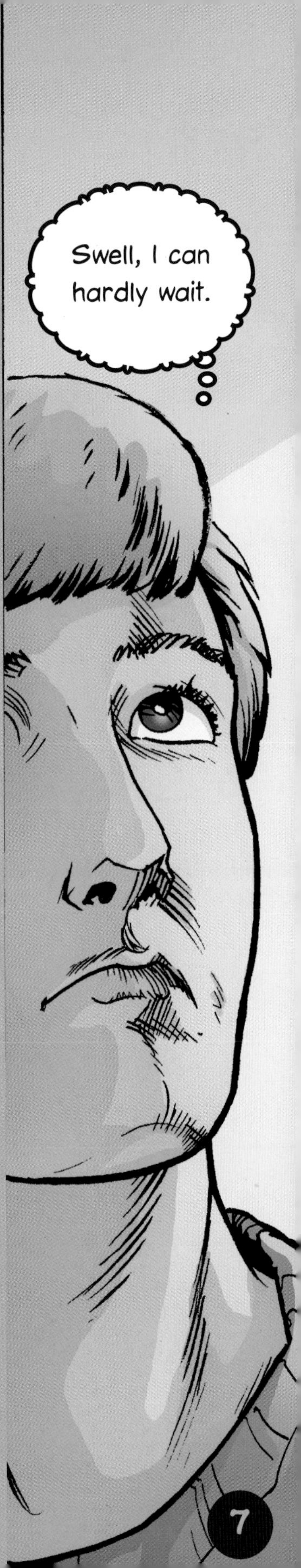
Swell, I can hardly wait.

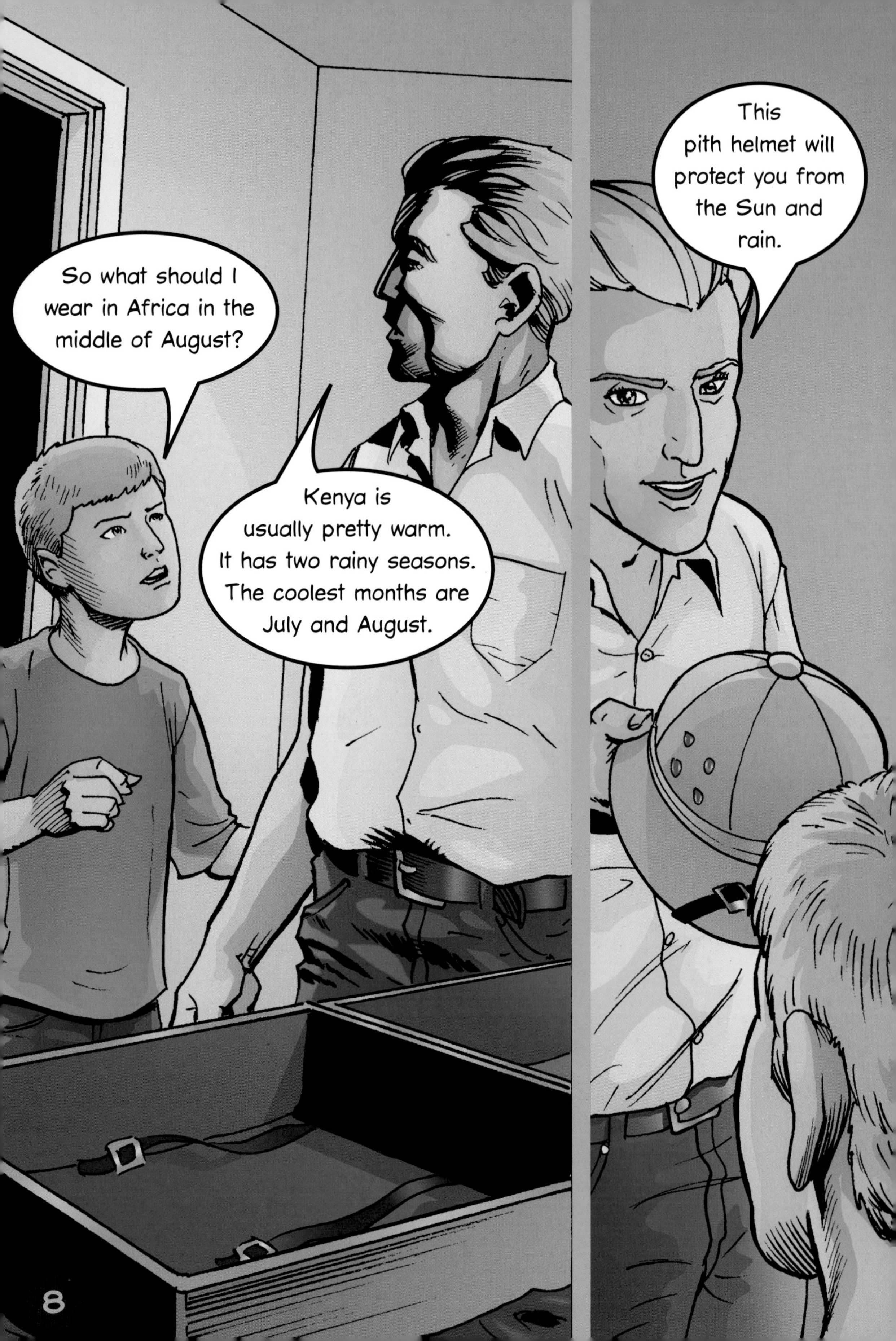
So what should I wear in Africa in the middle of August?
Kenya is usually pretty warm. It has two rainy seasons. The coolest months are July and August.
This pith helmet will protect you from the Sun and rain.

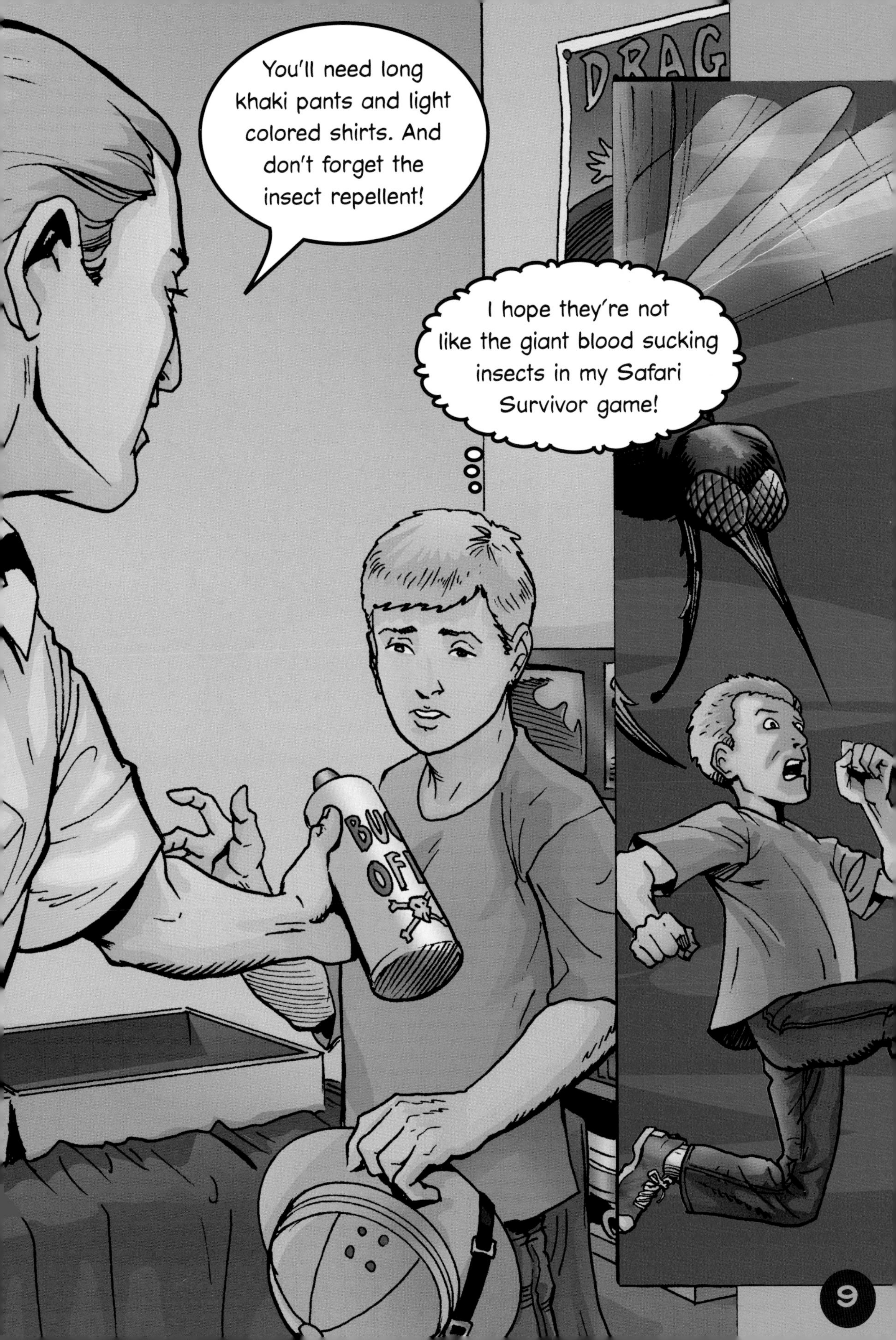

You'll need long khaki pants and light colored shirts. And don't forget the insect repellent!
I hope they're not like the giant blood sucking insects in my Safari Survivor game!
BUG OFF
DRAG

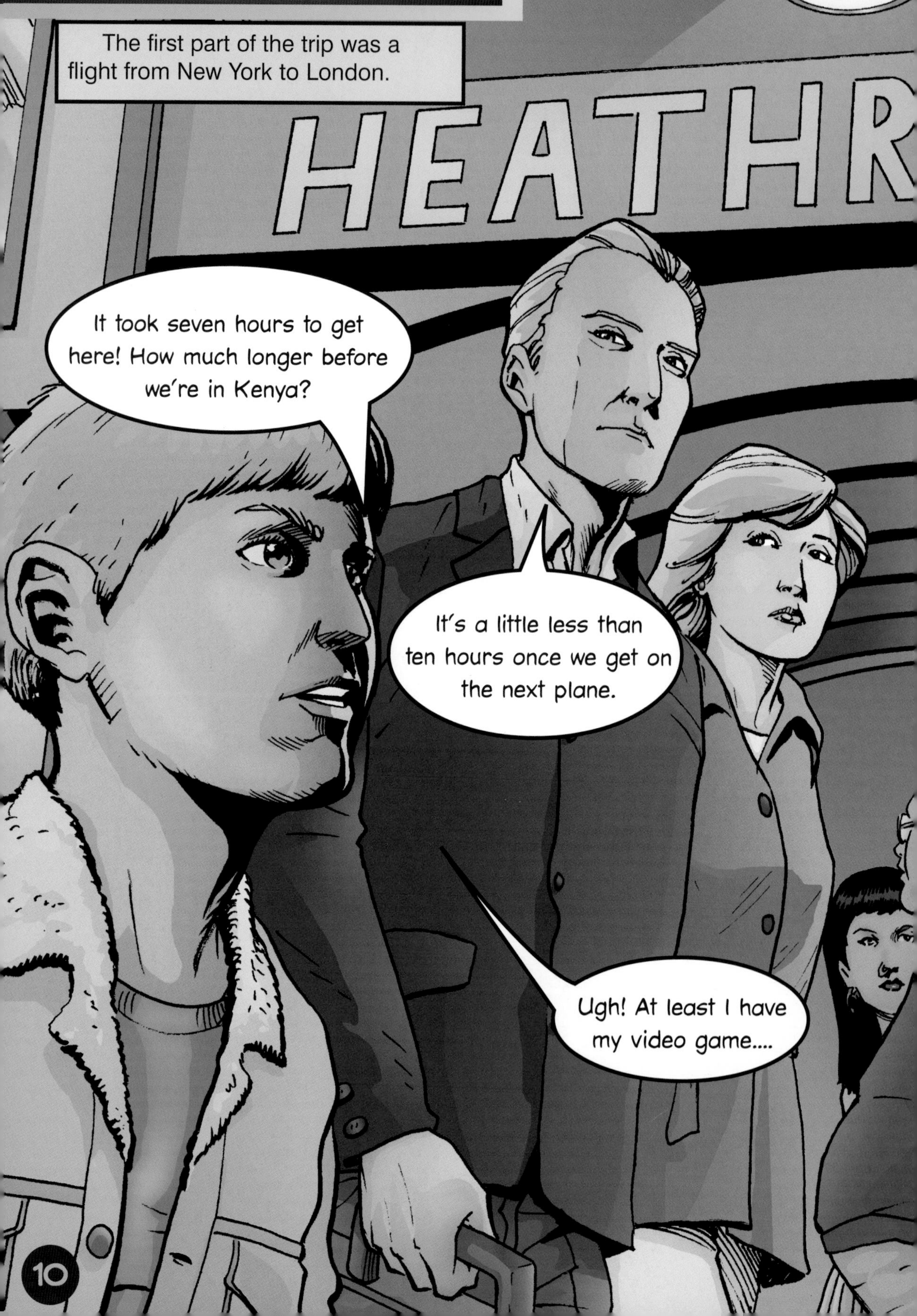
The first part of the trip was a flight from New York to London.
HEATHR
It took seven hours to get here! How much longer before we're in Kenya?
It's a little less than ten hours once we get on the next plane.
Ugh! At least I have my video game....

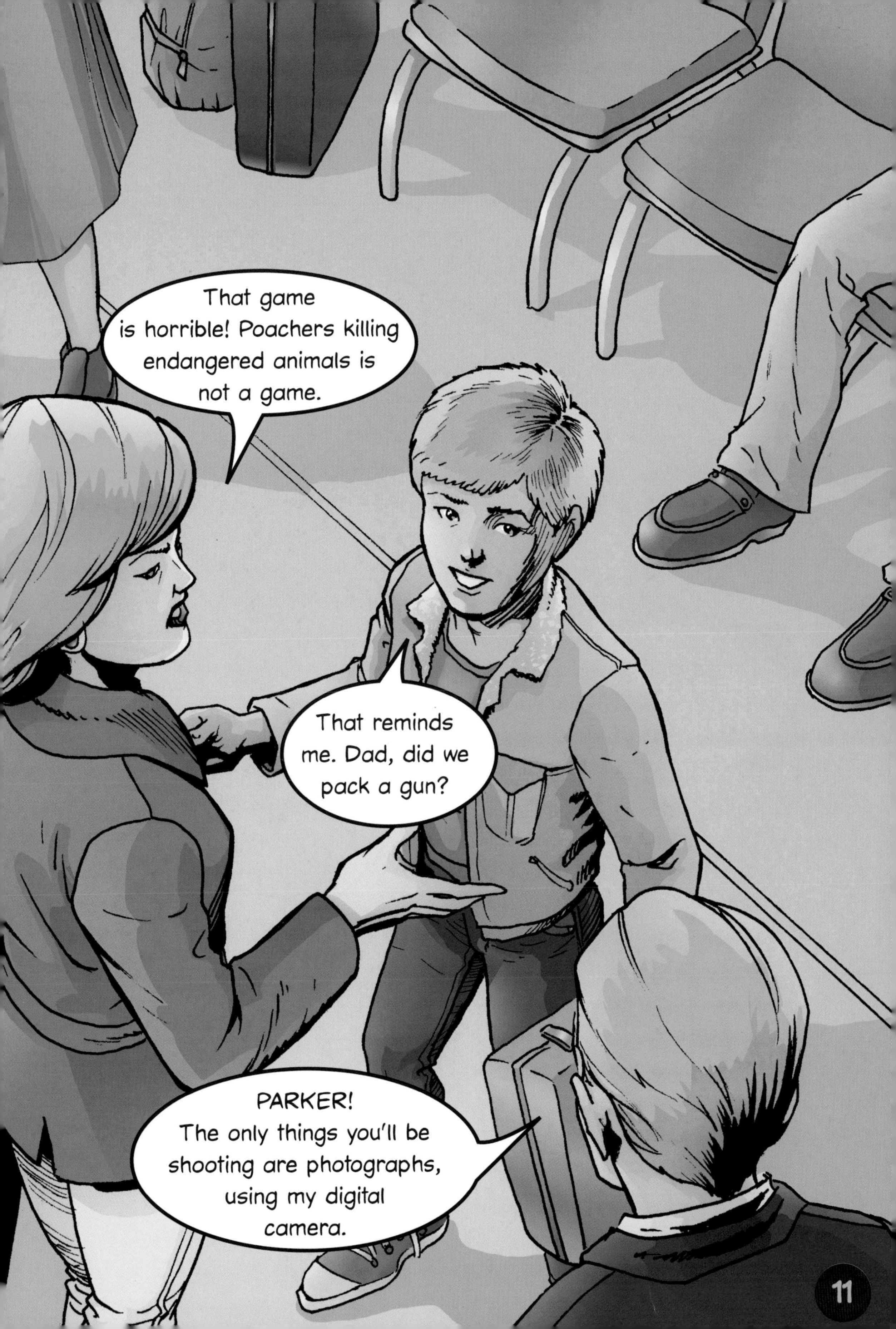
That game is horrible! Poachers killing endangered animals is not a game.
That reminds me. Dad, did we pack a gun?
PARKER! The only things you'll be shooting are photographs, using my digital camera.

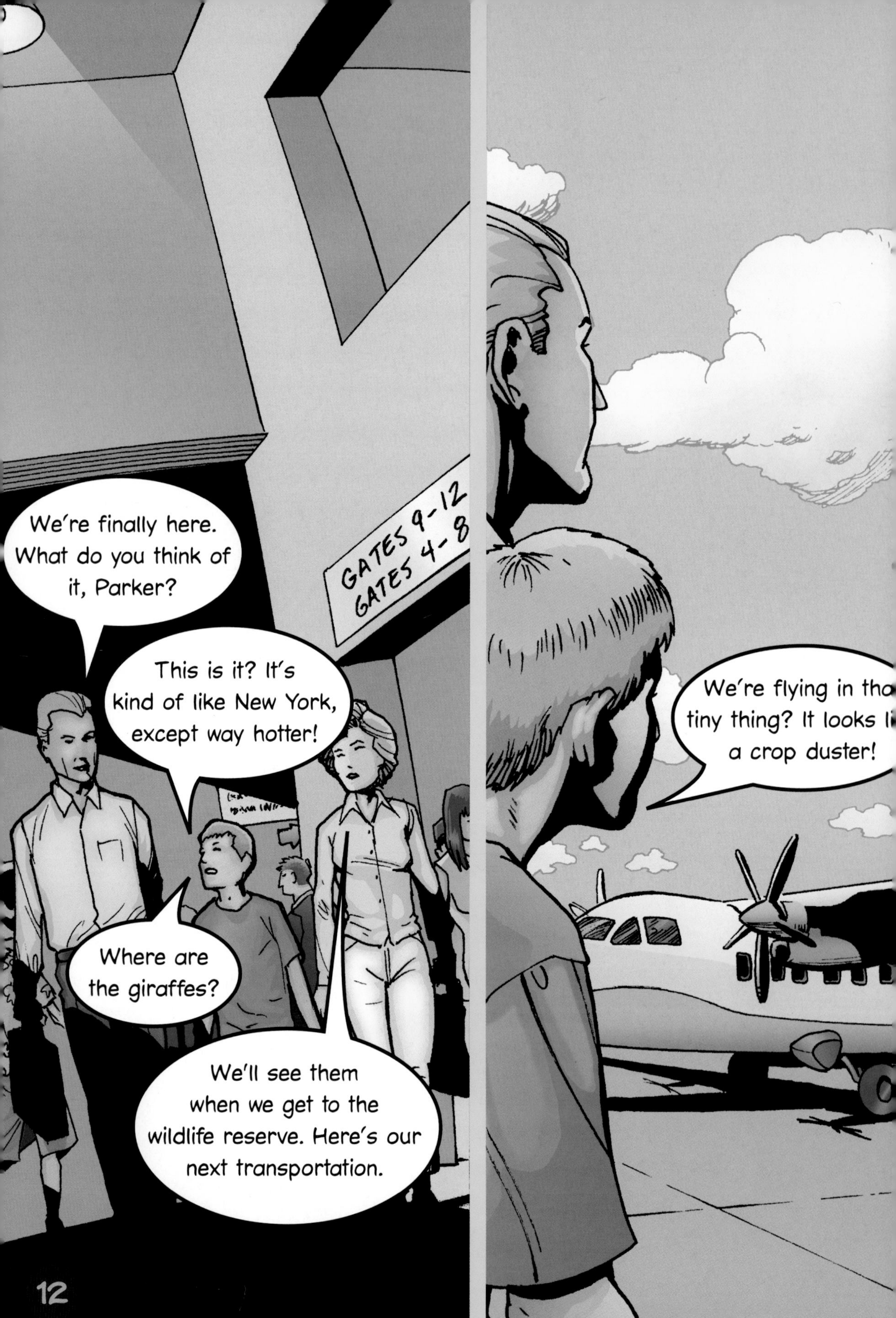
GATES 9-12
GATES 4-8
We're finally here. What do you think of it, Parker?
This is it? It's kind of like New York, except way hotter!
Where are the giraffes?
We'll see them when we get to the wildlife reserve. Here's our next transportation.
We're flying in tha tiny thing? It looks li a crop duster!

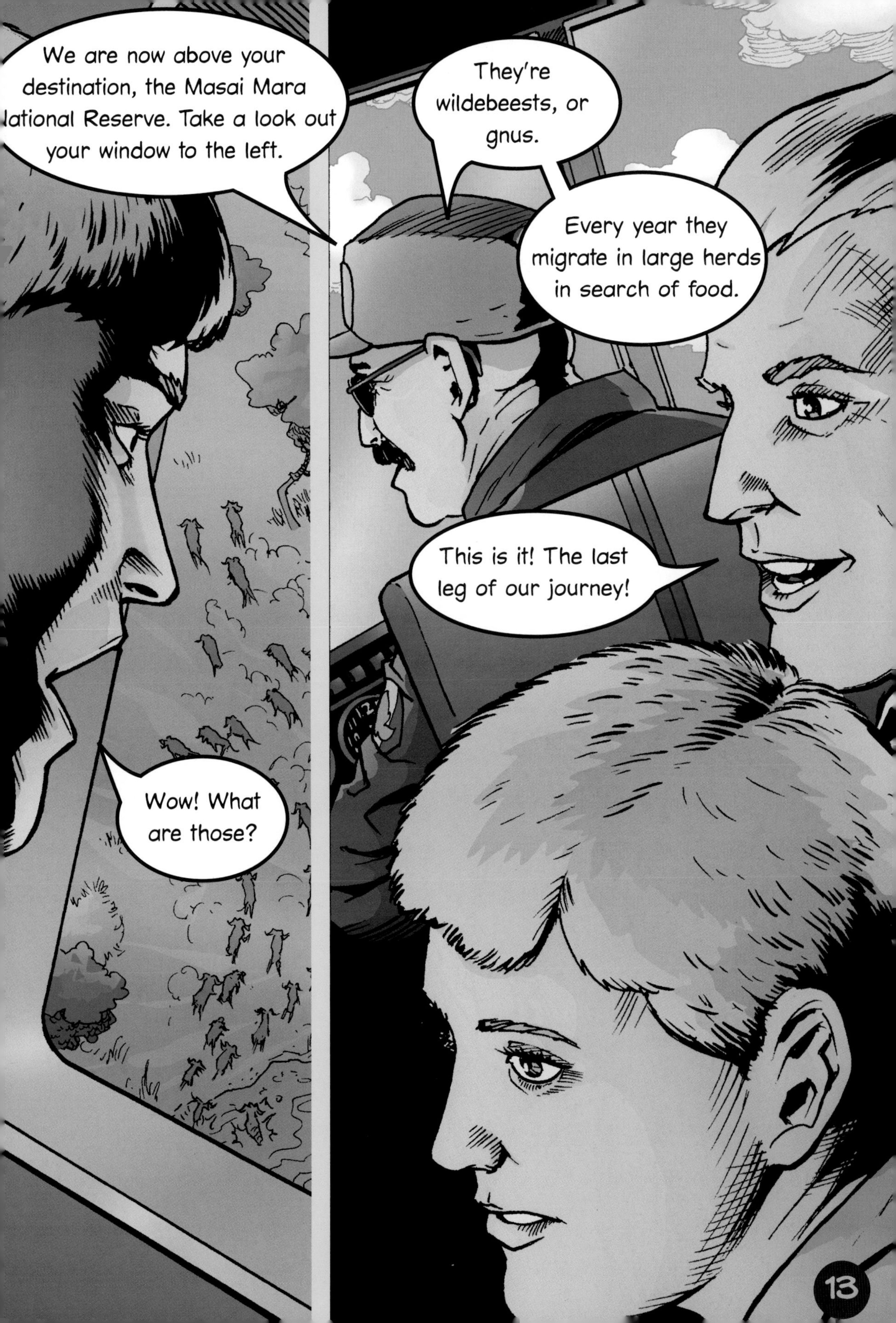
We are now above your destination, the Masai Mara lational Reserve. Take a look out your window to the left.
Wow! What are those?
They're wildebeests, or gnus.
Every year they migrate in large herds in search of food.
This is it! The last leg of our journey!

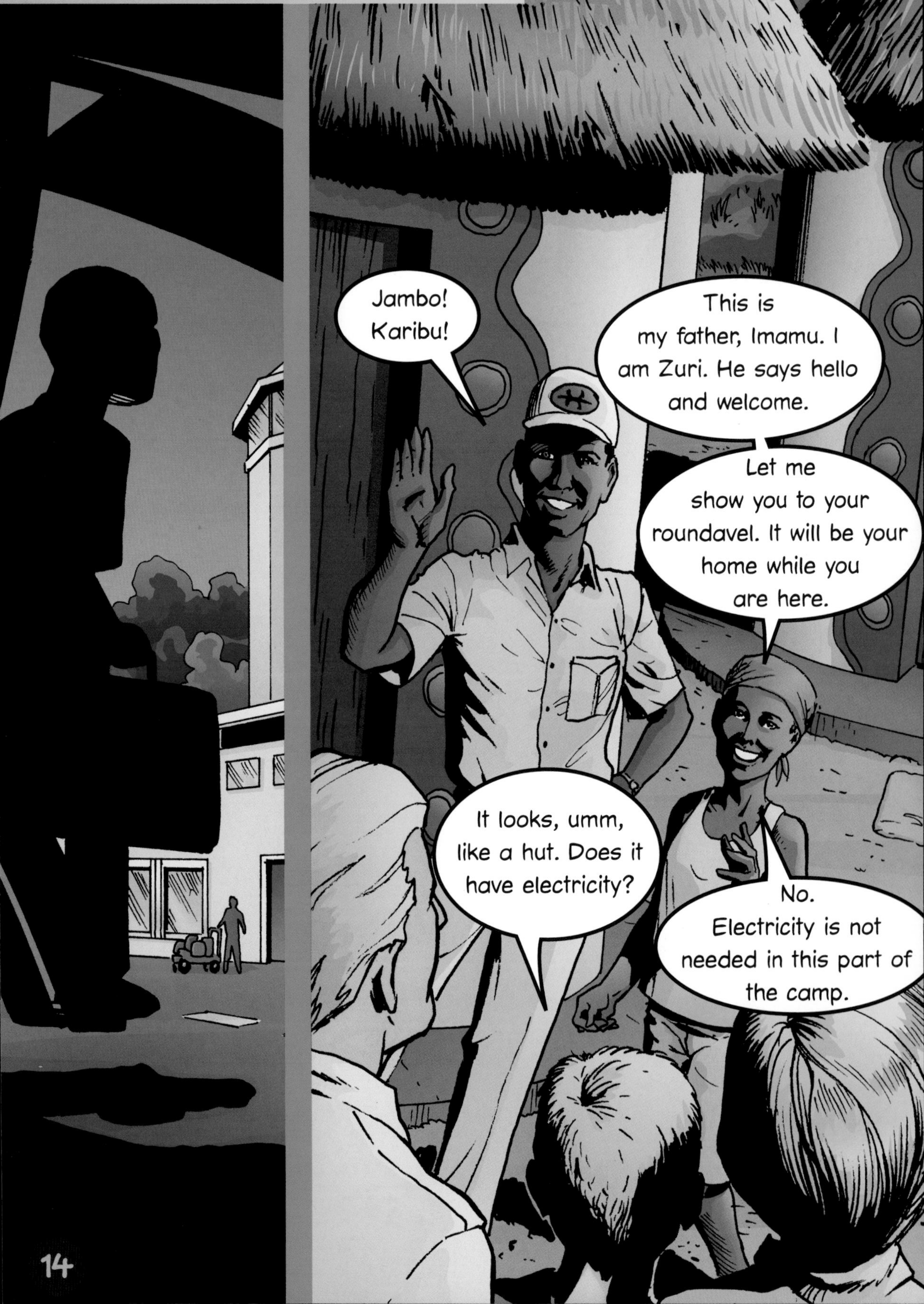
Jambo! Karibu!
This is my father, Imamu. I am Zuri. He says hello and welcome.
Let me show you to your roundavel. It will be your home while you are here.
It looks, umm, like a hut. Does it have electricity?
No. Electricity is not needed in this part of the camp.

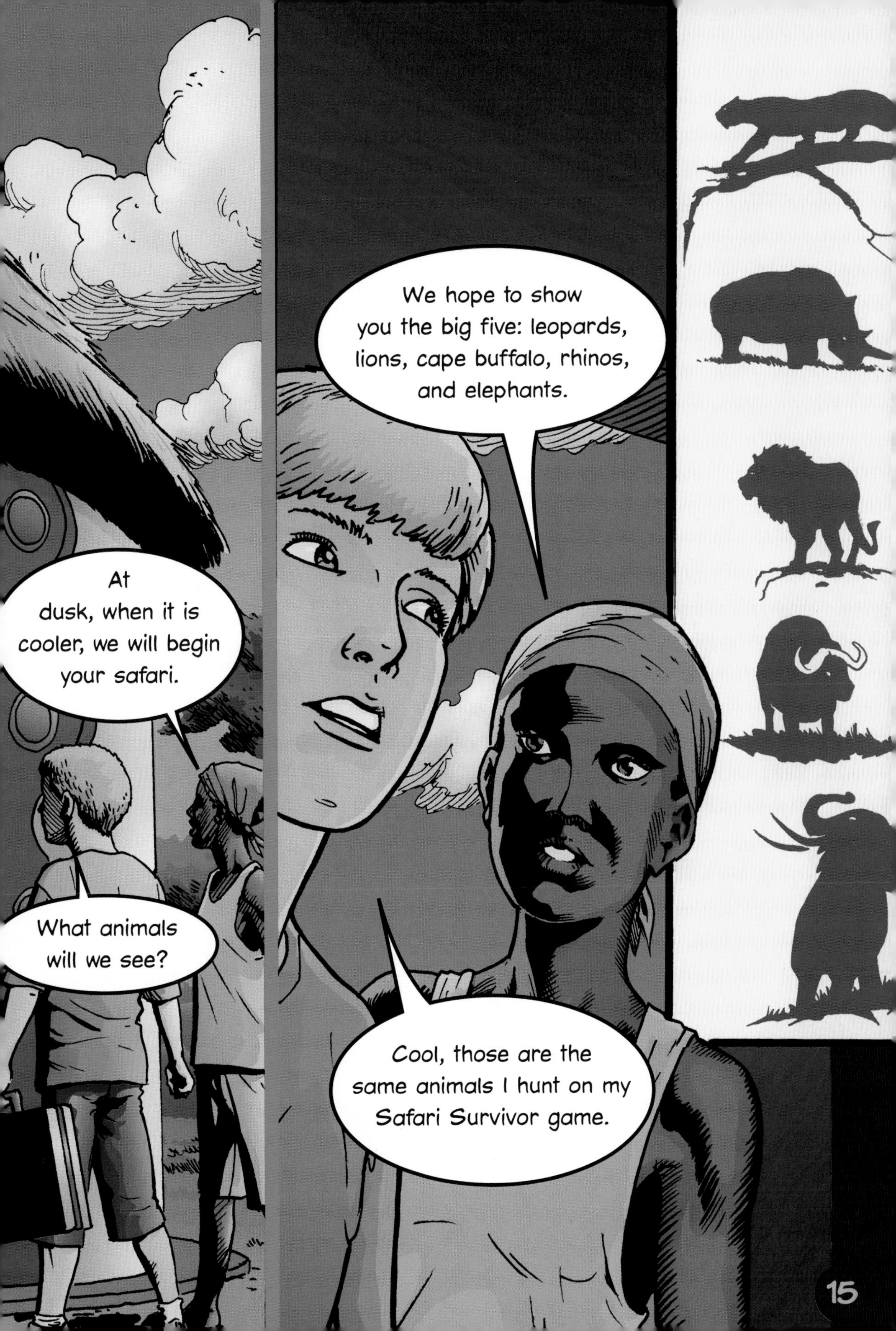
At dusk, when it is cooler, we will begin your safari.
What animals will we see?
We hope to show you the big five: leopards, lions, cape buffalo, rhinos, and elephants.
Cool, those are the same animals I hunt on my Safari Survivor game.

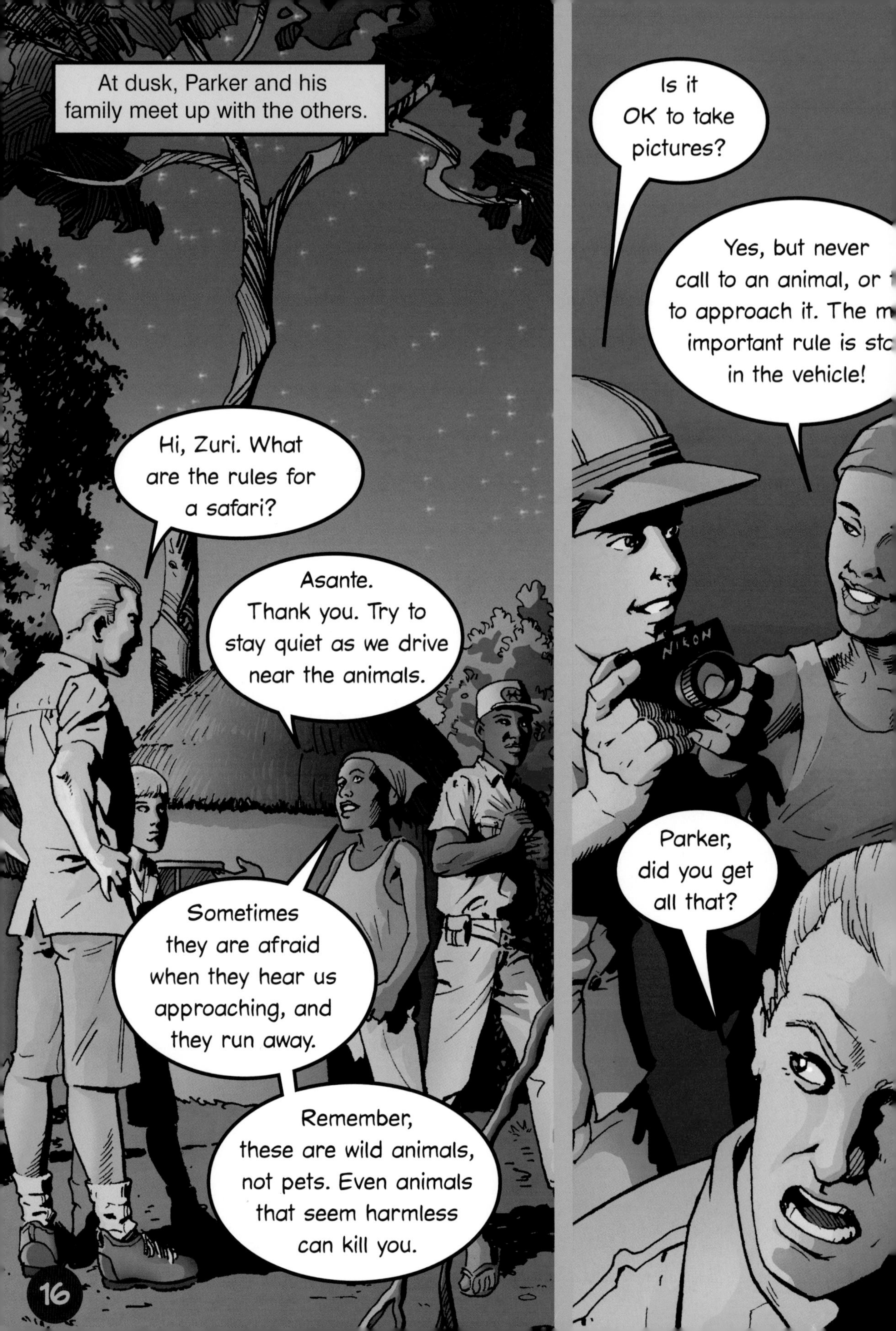
At dusk, Parker and his family meet up with the others.
Hi, Zuri. What are the rules for a safari?
Asante. Thank you. Try to stay quiet as we drive near the animals.
Sometimes they are afraid when they hear us approaching, and they run away.
Remember, these are wild animals, not pets. Even animals that seem harmless can kill you.
Is it OK to take pictures?
Yes, but never call to an animal, or to approach it. The important rule is in the vehicle!
Parker, did you get all that?

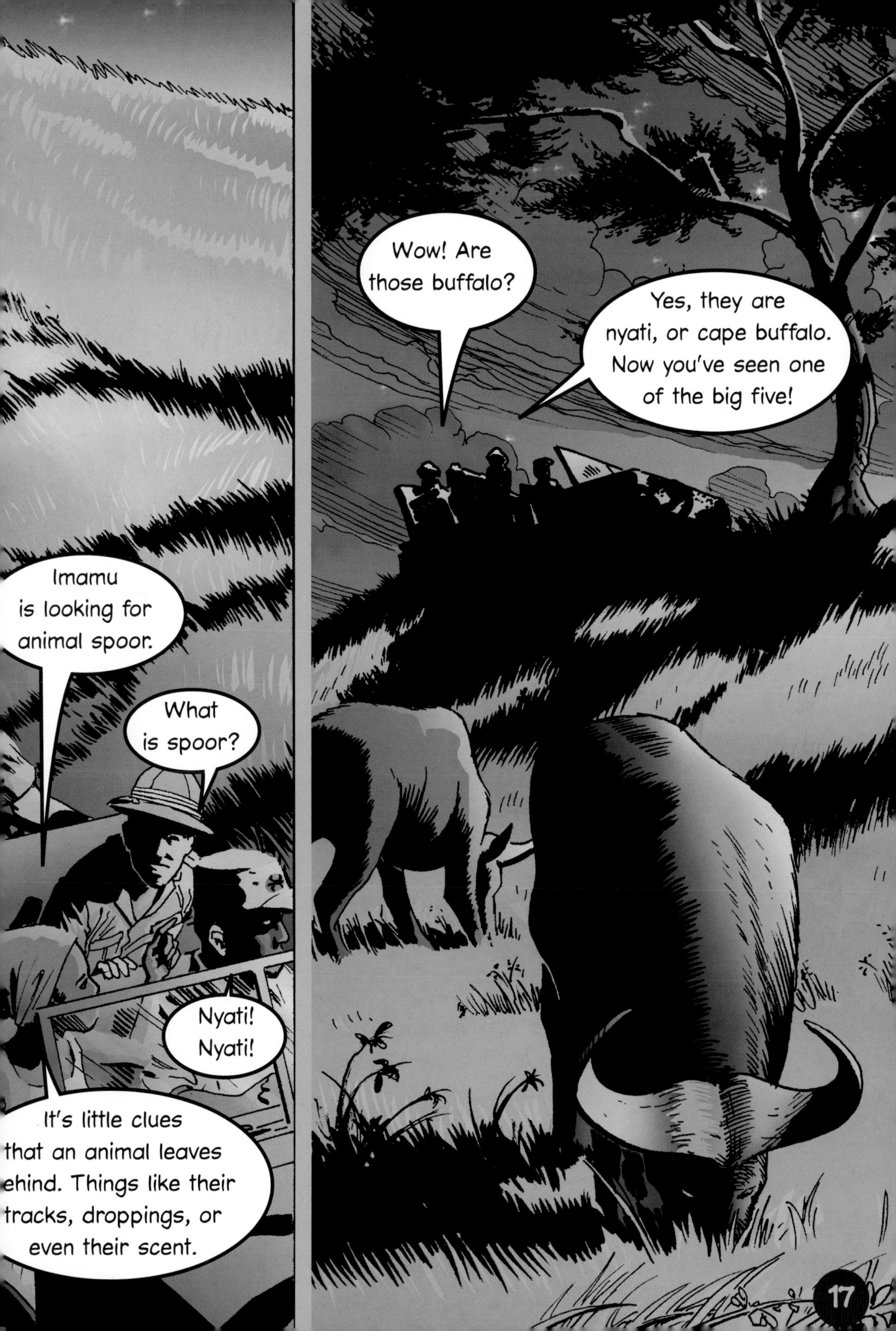
Imamu is looking for animal spoor.
What is spoor?
It's little clues that an animal leaves ehind. Things like their tracks, droppings, or even their scent.
Nyati! Nyati!
Wow! Are those buffalo?
Yes, they are nyati, or cape buffalo. Now you've seen one of the big five!

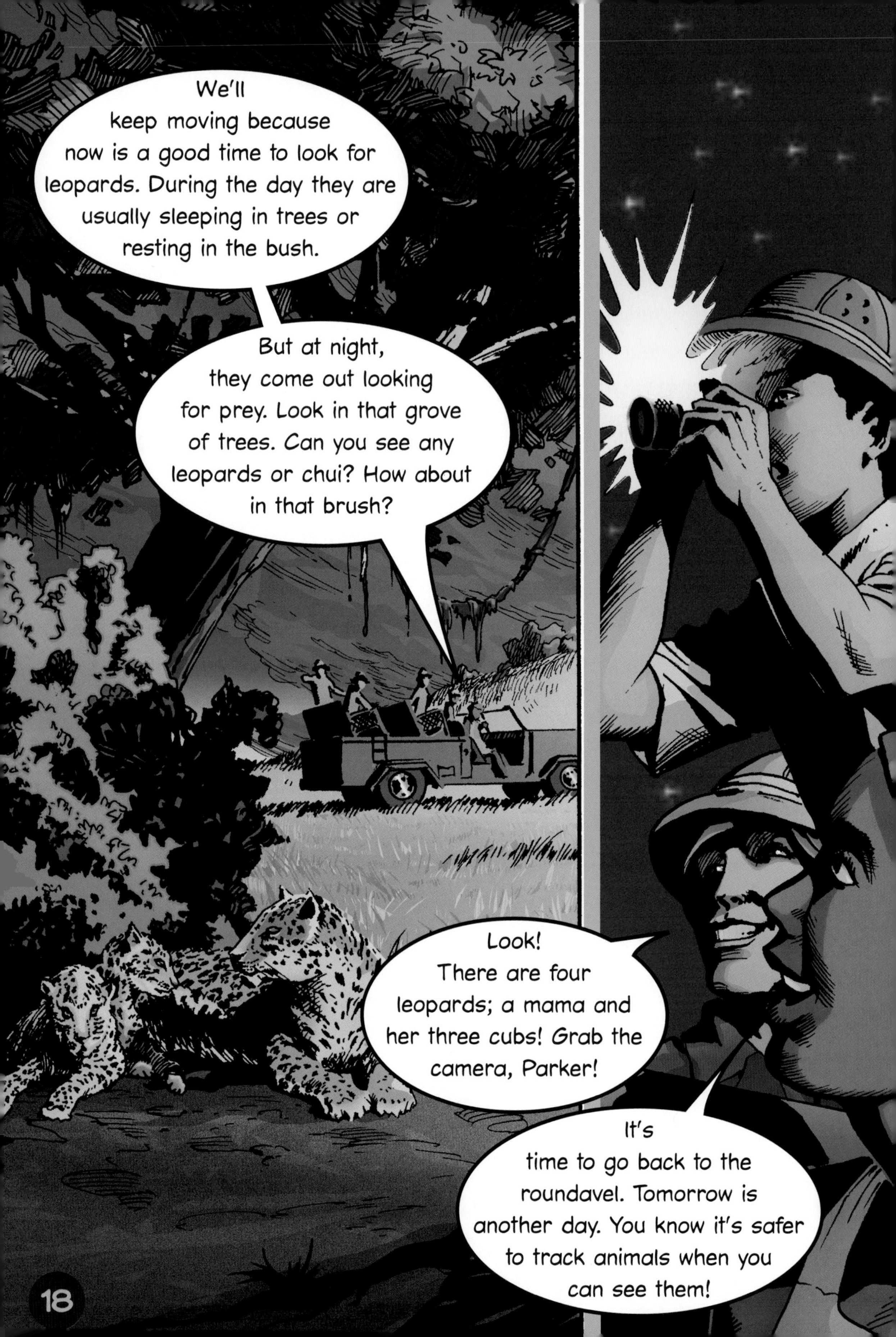
We'll keep moving because now is a good time to look for leopards. During the day they are usually sleeping in trees or resting in the bush.
But at night, they come out looking for prey. Look in that grove of trees. Can you see any leopards or chui? How about in that brush?
Look! There are four leopards; a mama and her three cubs! Grab the camera, Parker!
It's time to go back to the roundavel. Tomorrow is another day. You know it's safer to track animals when you can see them!

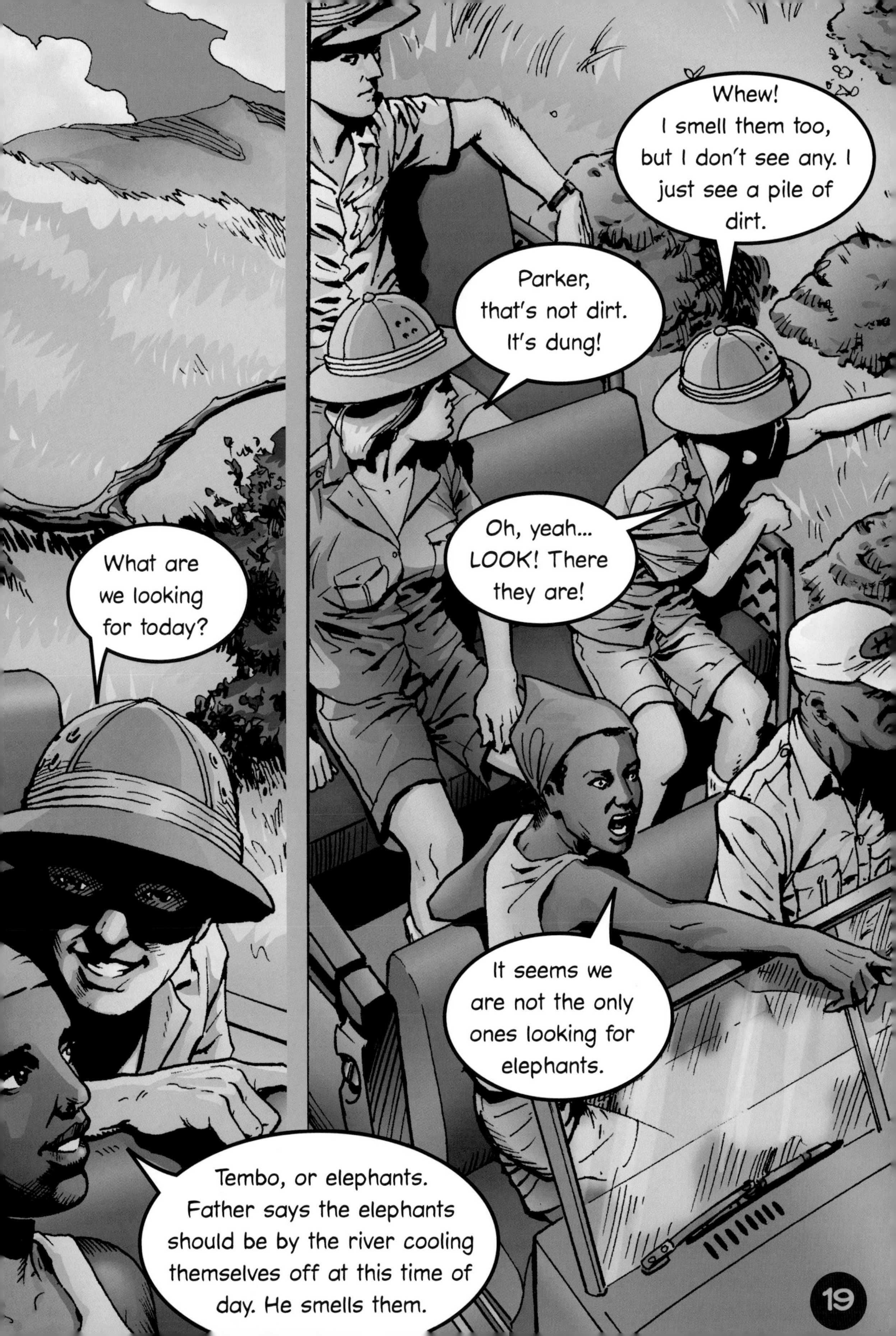
What are we looking for today?
Tembo, or elephants. Father says the elephants should be by the river cooling themselves off at this time of day. He smells them.
Whew! I smell them too, but I don't see any. I just see a pile of dirt.
Parker, that's not dirt. It's dung!
Oh, yeah... LOOK! There they are!
It seems we are not the only ones looking for elephants.

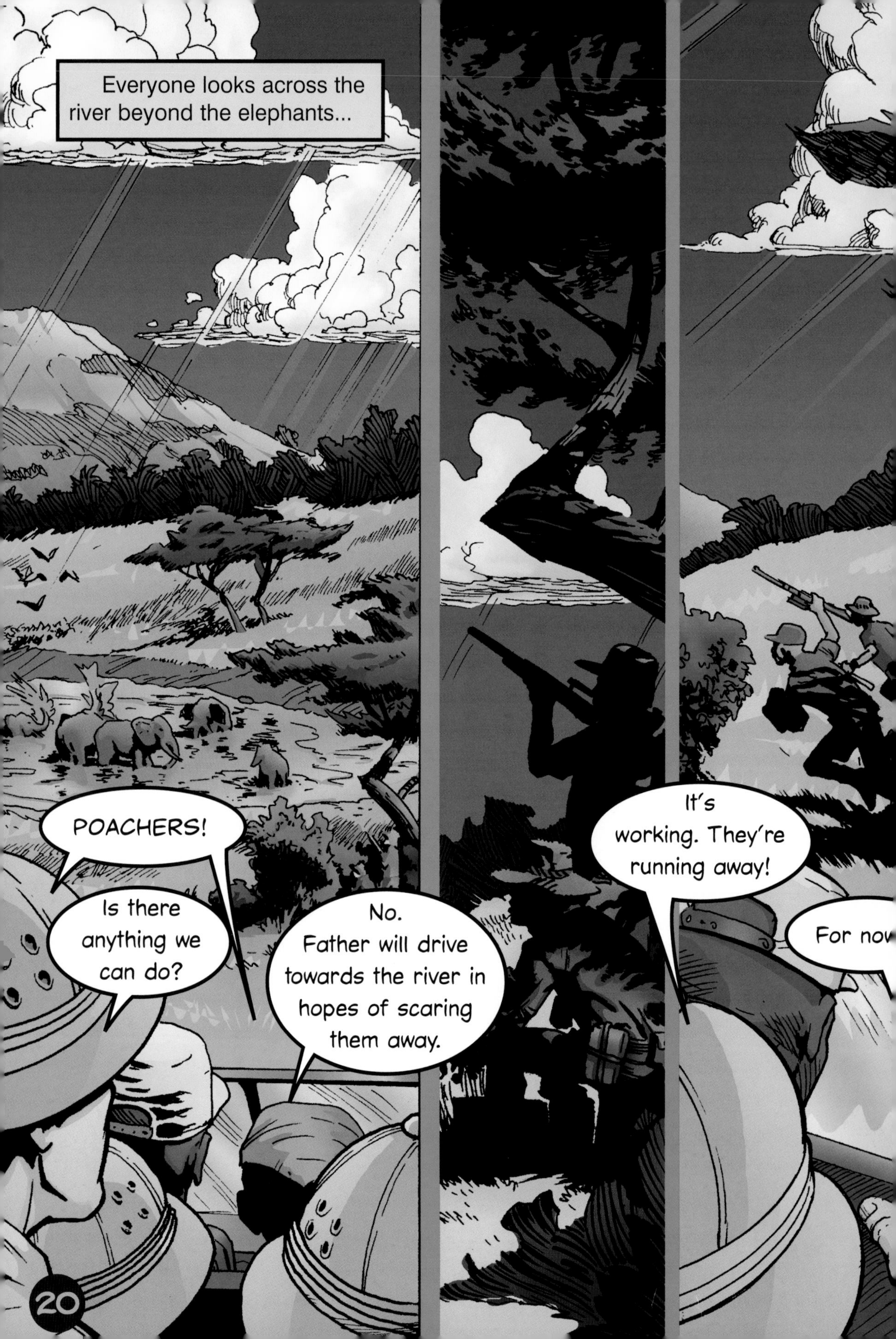
Everyone looks across the river beyond the elephants...
POACHERS!
Is there anything we can do?
No. Father will drive towards the river in hopes of scaring them away.
It's working. They're running away!
For no

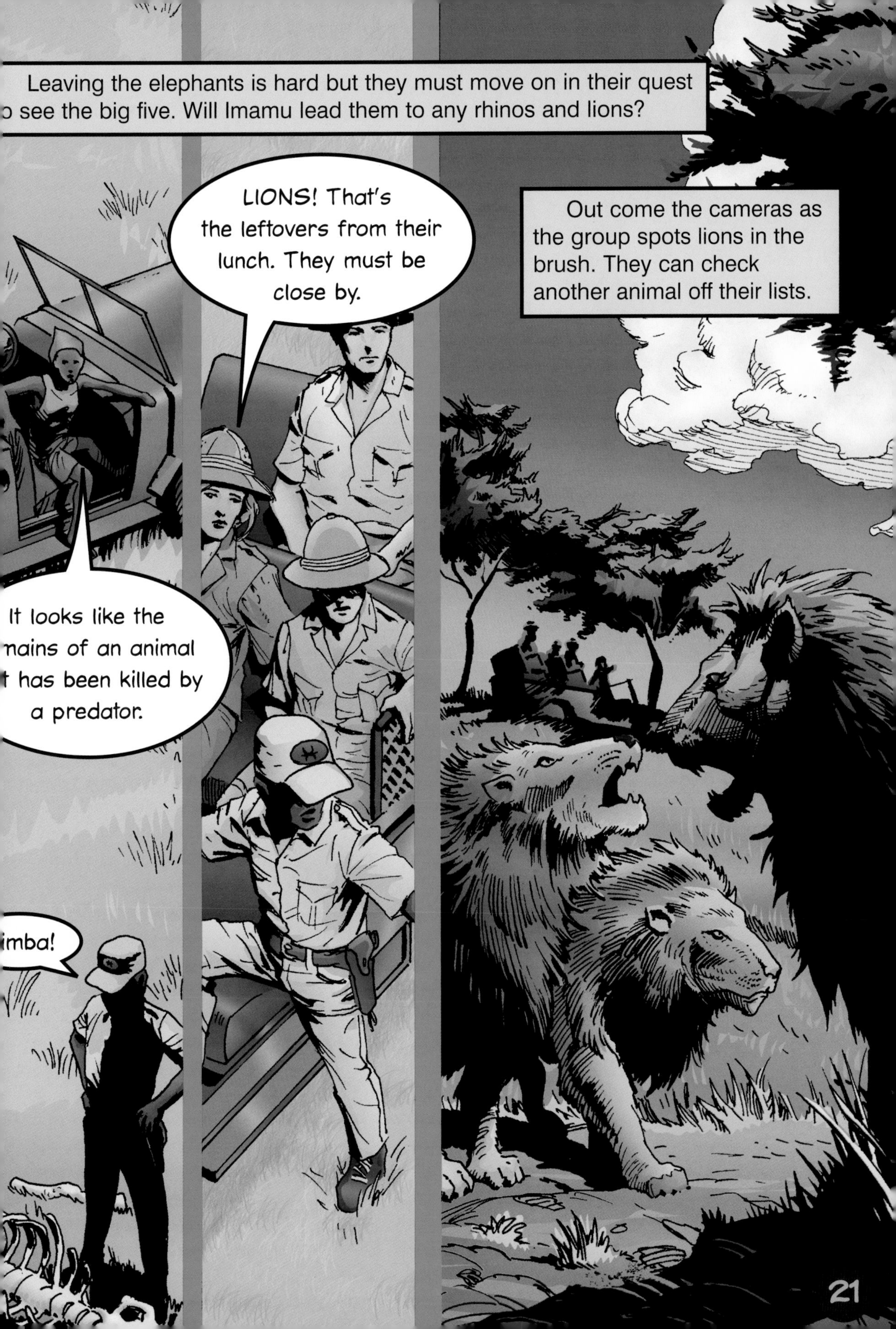
Leaving the elephants is hard but they must move on in their quest o see the big five. Will Imamu lead them to any rhinos and lions?
It looks like the nains of an animal t has been killed by a predator.
imba!
LIONS! That's the leftovers from their lunch. They must be close by.
Out come the cameras as the group spots lions in the brush. They can check another animal off their lists.

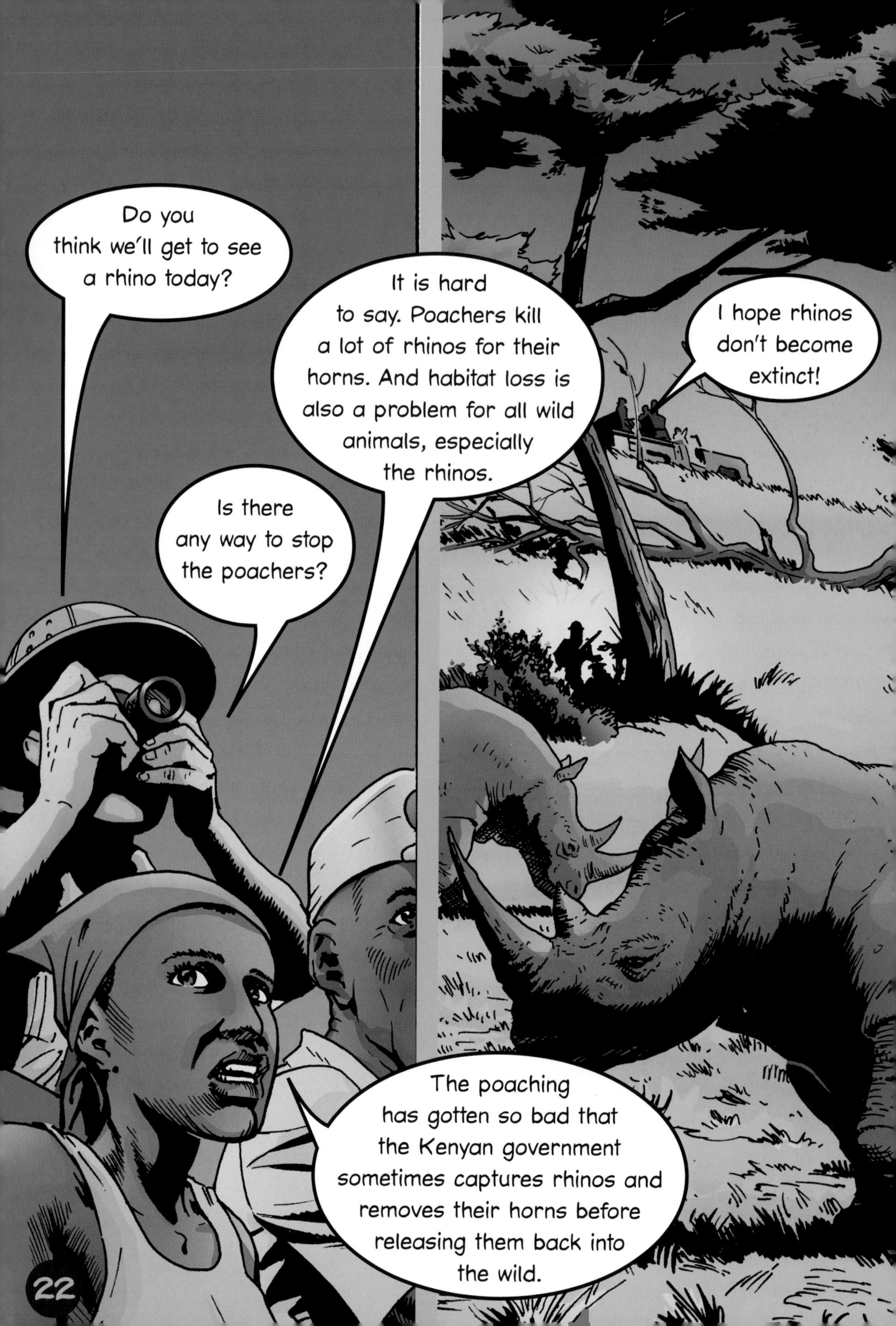
Do you think we'll get to see a rhino today?
It is hard to say. Poachers kill a lot of rhinos for their horns. And habitat loss is also a problem for all wild animals, especially the rhinos.
I hope rhinos don't become extinct!
Is there any way to stop the poachers?
The poaching has gotten so bad that the Kenyan government sometimes captures rhinos and removes their horns before releasing them back into the wild.

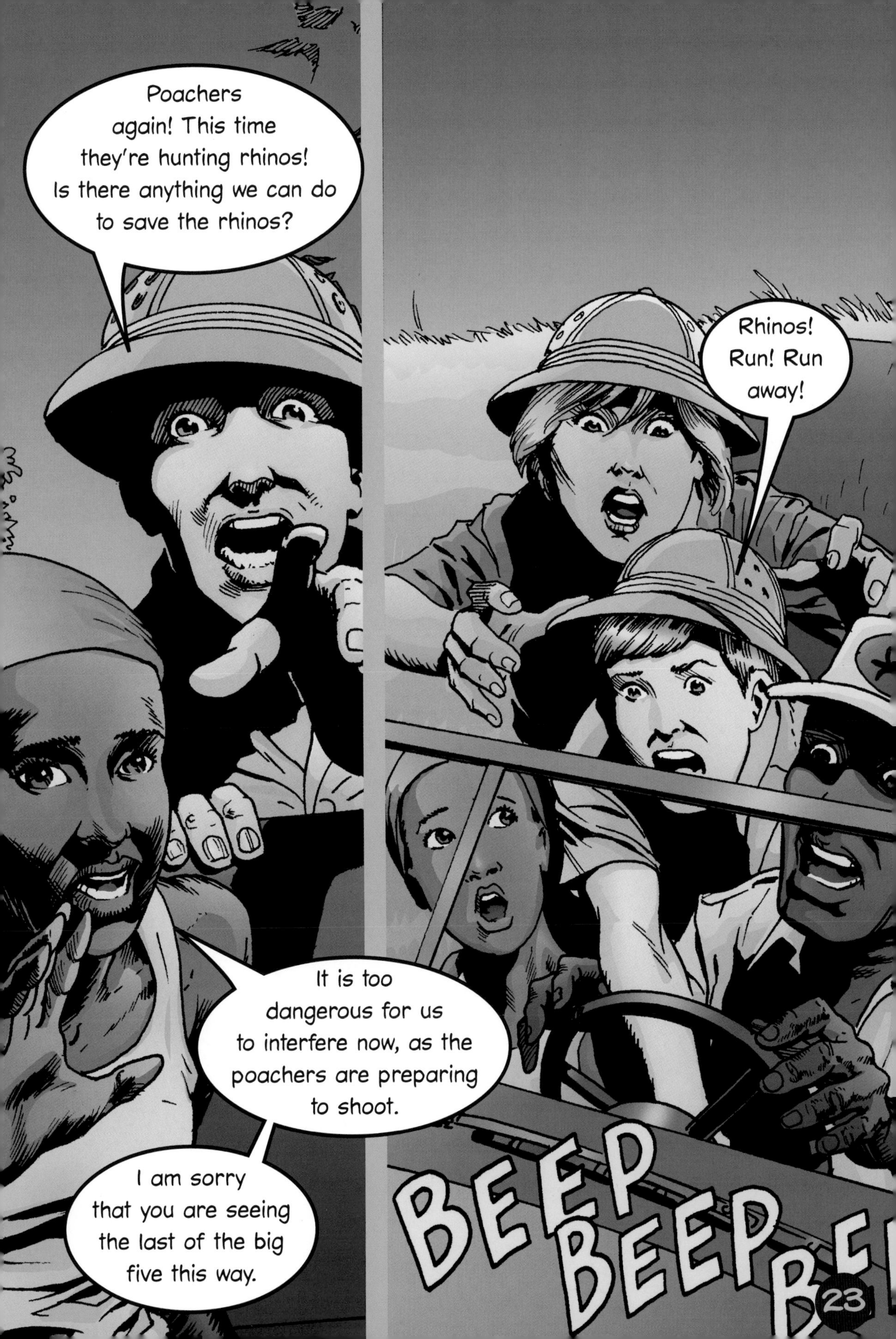
Poachers again! This time they're hunting rhinos! Is there anything we can do to save the rhinos?
It is too dangerous for us to interfere now, as the poachers are preparing to shoot.
I am sorry that you are seeing the last of the big five this way.
Rhinos! Run! Run away!
BEEP
BEEP

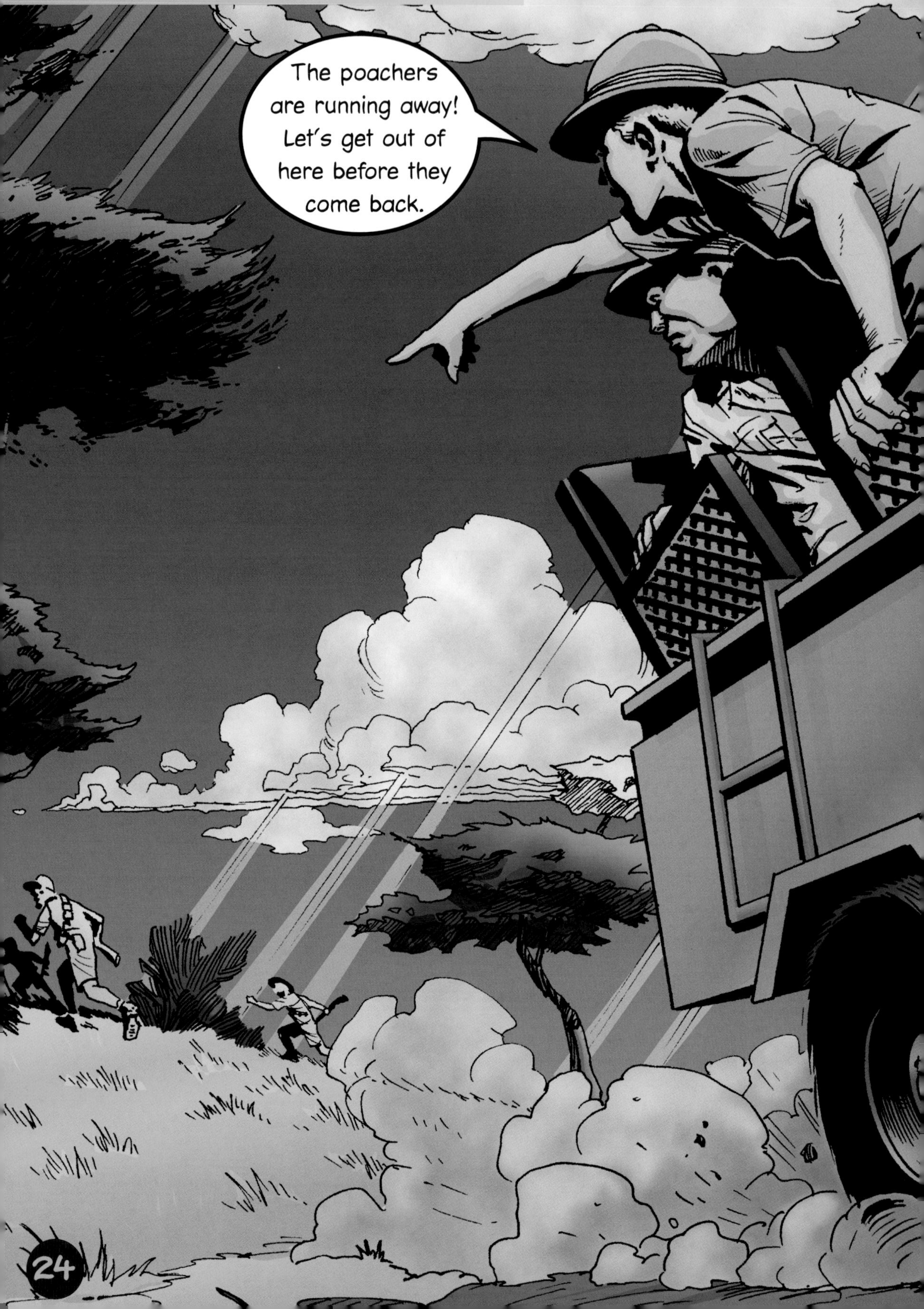
The poachers are running away! Let's get out of here before they come back.

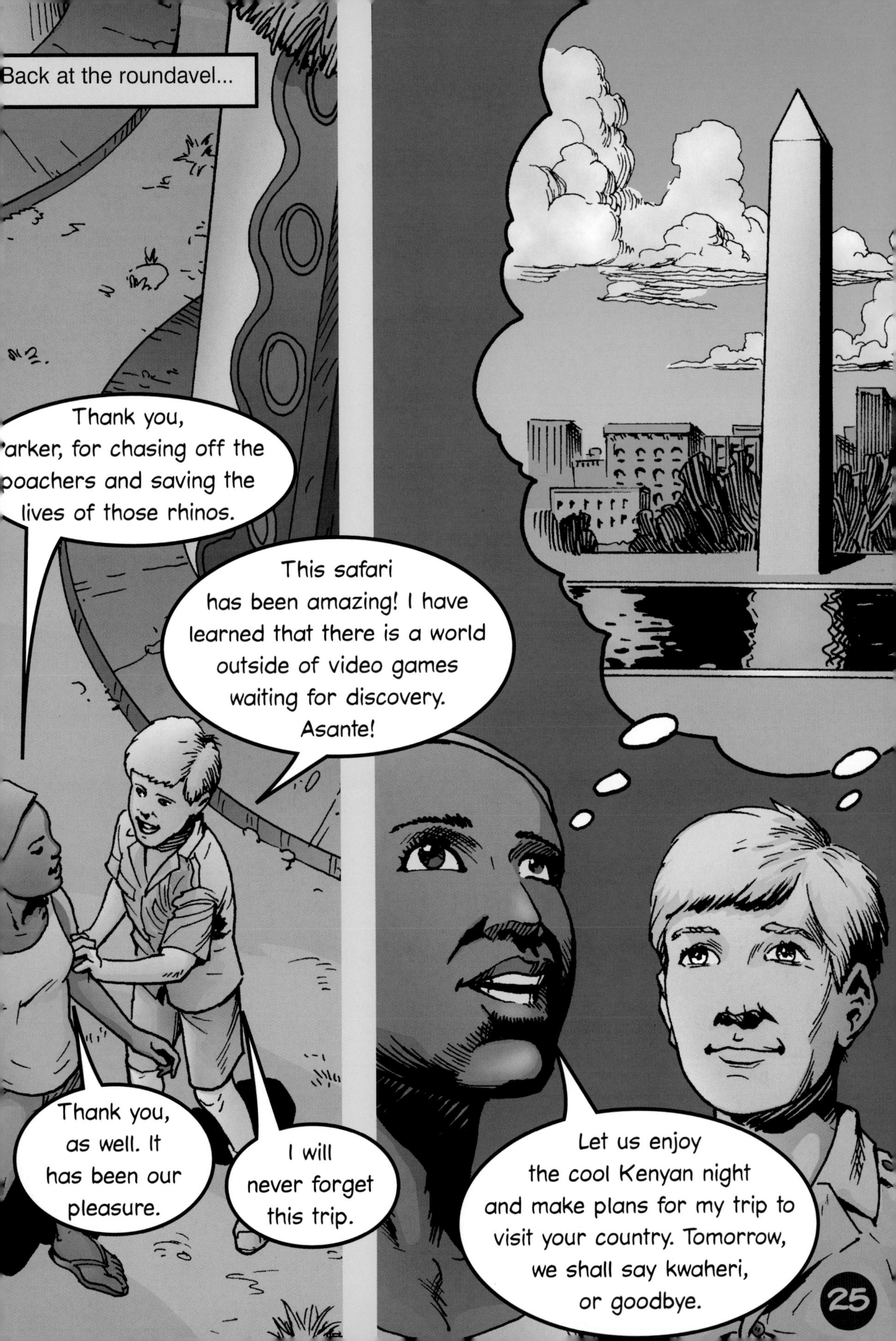

Back at the roundavel...
Thank you, arker, for chasing off the poachers and saving the lives of those rhinos.
This safari has been amazing! I have learned that there is a world outside of video games waiting for discovery. Asante!
Thank you, as well. It has been our pleasure.
I will never forget this trip.
Let us enjoy the cool Kenyan night and make plans for my trip to visit your country. Tomorrow, we shall say kwaheri, or goodbye.

The Big Five

Common Name	Scientific Name	Typical Size	Number Remaining	Interesting Facts
African or Cape Buffalo 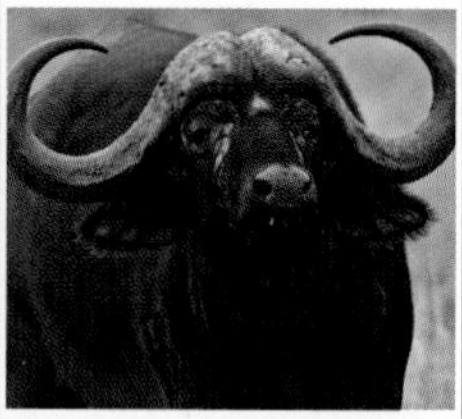	Synerus caffer	3 to 6 feet (1 to 2 meters) tall and 900 to 2,000 pounds (408 to 907 kilograms)	About 1 million	Older buffalo spend a lot of time in the mud to keep flies and parasites away. These bulls are called dagga boys. Dagga means mud.
African Elephant 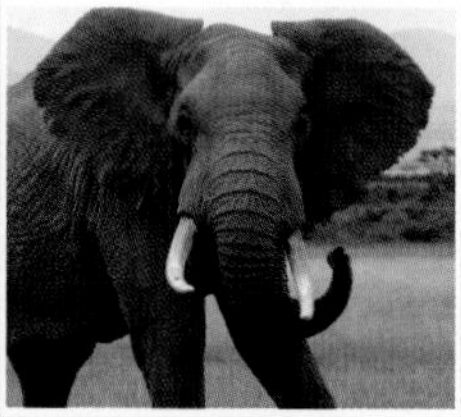	Loxodonta	12 feet (4 meters) tall and 12,000 pounds (5,443 kilograms)	About 500,000	These are the heaviest land animals. Their ears can reach 4 feet (1.2 meters) across
Leopard 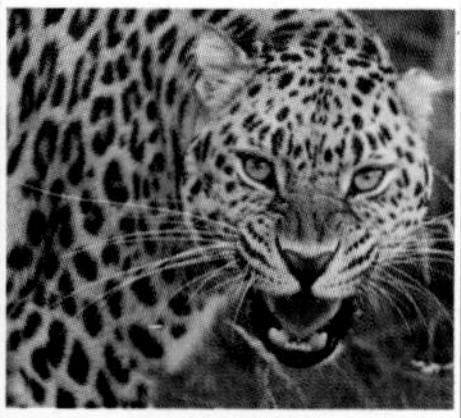	Panthera pardus	Up to 6 feet (2 meters) long and 200 pounds (91 kilograms)	About 500,000	Leopards can climb trees. They sometimes carry their food up a tree to avoid competition with lions and other big cats.
Lion 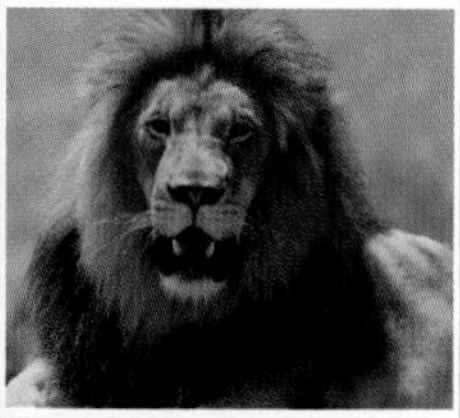	Panthera leo	From 6 to 8 feet (2 to 2.4 meters) in length and up to 500 pounds (227 kilograms)	About 25,000	The male lion is the only cat with a mane. The lioness has no mane.
Rhino 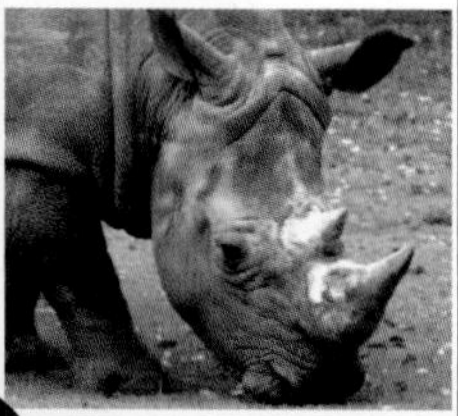	Ceratotherium simum (White Rhino) and Diceros bicornis (Black Rhino)	About 5 feet (1.5 meters) tall and up to 4,000 pounds (1,814 kilograms)	About 10,000	Rhinos have very poor vision and will often charge moving objects. African rhinos have two horns.

There are many places to go on a safari in Africa. Each of the wildlife parks highlighted below contains all of the big five animals.

Botswana—Moremi Wildlife Reserve
Kenya—Masai Mara National Reserve
Namibia—Etosha National Park
South Africa—Kruger National Park
Tanzania—Serengeti National Park

Ethiopia
Central Africa Republic
Cameroon
Somalia
Uganda
Kenya
Dem Republic of Congo
Gabon
Congo
Rwanda
Burundi
Tanzania
Indian Ocean
Seychelles
Comoros
Angola
Malawi
Zambia
Mozambique
Mozambique Channel
Madagascar
Namibia
Zimbabwe
Botswana
Swaziland
Lesotho
South Africa

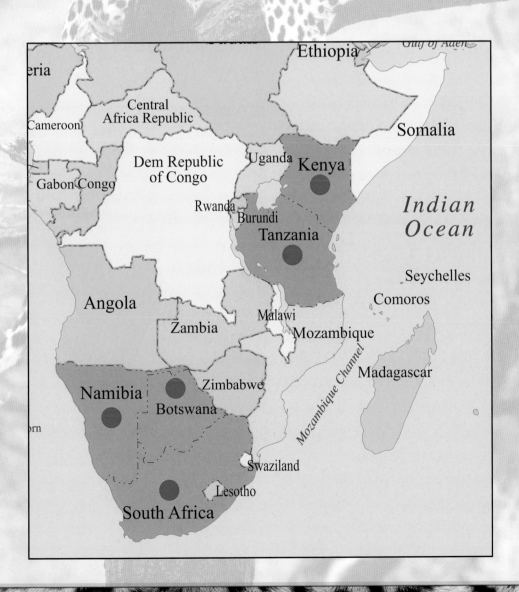

The Masai Mara National Reserve is the setting of this book and the largest wildlife reserve in Kenya. It covers about 700 square miles (1,813 square kilometers).

While the reserve does contain the big five, there is an abundant amount of other wildlife to see as well. On safari, you might also see hippos, zebras, giraffes, hyenas, and Thomson's gazelles. Some visitors have even had the amazing opportunity of seeing a cheetah or lion hunting and capturing their prey!

Known for its large number of lions, the Masai Mara is named for its people. The typical spelling when referring to the people is Maasai. They are a semi-nomadic tribe who make their living herding and selling livestock. They often go to towns and cities to sell their cattle and purchase goods they need. When tourists visit their villages, many have the opportunity to see traditional dances and clothing, and to purchase the beautiful beadwork they are famous for.

Wildebeests migrate every year between the Masai Mara and the Serengeti National Park in Tanzania.

The Maasai people have been able to maintain a traditional way of life, including the way they dress.

Maasai children have many chores in their villages. Girls are expected to assist in building the dung hut, milk the cows, and get the water. Boys are considered men at the age of fifteen. Part of the ritual used to include hunting and killing a lion. This practice is now illegal. Children also participate in rituals such as rainmaking, by singing for the rains to come. They enjoy playing a game called sheeps and goats, which is similar to cops and robbers.

Websites

www.africanculturalcenter.org

www.earthsendangered.com

www.kidsplanet.org/factsheets/map.html

www.game-reserve.com/kenya_masai-mara.html

www.kenyatravelideas.com/kenya-animals.html

Glossary

endangered (en-DAYN-jurd): If something is endangered, it is threatened. An endangered species is a type of animal or plant that is in danger of becoming extinct.

extinct (ek-STINGKT): When a plant or an animal species has died out, and there are no more on Earth, it is considered to be extinct.

habitat (HAB-uh-tat): A habitat is the place where a plant or animal lives.

migrate (MYE-grate): To migrate means to move from one place, or region, to another. When a bird migrates, it flies from a particular climate to another one during a particular time of year.

poachers (POHCH-urs): People who hunt or fish in areas where it is illegal to do so.

predator (PRED-uh-tur): A predator is an animal that hunts other animals for food.

repellent (ri-PEL-uhnt): A repellent is a special chemical that is used to keep insects and other pests away.

reserve (ri-ZURV): A reserve is a special place set aside for animals so that they are protected. They can live and breed safely at the reserve.

safari (suh-FAH-ree): A safari is a trip that a person takes to another place, such as Africa, to see large, wild animals in their natural habitats.

wildlife (WILDE-life): Wildlife are animals living in their natural environment. These animals are wild or untamed.

Index

About the Author

Tim Clifford is an education writer and the author of many nonfiction children's books. He has two wonderful daughters and two energetic Border Collies that he adopted from a shelter. Tim became a vegetarian because of his love for animals. He is also a  computer nut and a sports fanatic. He lives and works in New York City as a public school teacher.

About the Artists

Ken Hooper has been a professional artist since 1985 when he embarked on a career in comics. His list of comic art include Swamp Thing, Aquaman, Star Trek, Indiana Jones, Elfquest, and Primal Force, to name a few.

Lance Borde earned his degree in English and Fine Arts through the university system in his home state of California. His career includes work in the arts and in graphics and design.